Baby's First Year
Journal and Prayer Book

Baby's First Year

Journal and Prayer Book

My Thoughts, Hopes and Prayers for You that First Year

Xulon Press

Xulon Press
2301 Lucien Way #415
Maitland, FL 32751
407.339.4217
www.xulonpress.com

© 2019 by Patricia Hull

All rights reserved solely by the author. The author guarantees all contents are original and do not infringe upon the legal rights of any other person or work. No part of this book may wbe reproduced in any form without the permission of the author. The views expressed in this book are not necessarily those of the publisher.

Unless otherwise indicated, Scripture quotations taken from the New King James Version (NKJV). Copyright © 1982 by Thomas Nelson, Inc. Used by permission. All rights reserved.

Printed in the United States of America.

ISBN-13: 978-1-54565-965-6

AUTHOR'S PERSPECTIVE

You have before you a thirty year endeavor. I wrote these poetic expressions during the first year I was a mother. I am just now putting them into a journal for others to use. I was very blessed to be able to be home with my baby during that first year and it happened that God gave me verses to write down concerning the transitions my child and I went through as we grew up together.

How can anyone look at a baby and not think that there is a God? When they are first born, infants are amazing to look at. The intricacies of their form are beyond expression. Of course, life is amazing in its creation and our children are always amazing to us parents.

As you enter this first year of life with your newborn, **make** the time to be alone with your child. Each day that you are able to do this, take a page of this journal, read the poem, the scripture and the prayer. Then just rest and allow God to give you *your own* prayer, thought, expression or whatever comes to mind that you can write down. There are additional pages at the end of the journal for you to write more or to save pictures and other mementos. Be sure to date the page. Since there are not 365 entries, be creative if you do write every day. Add pages as you need to. One day when your child is grown, you can give him or her this journal. What they can't remember, they will be able to read, about how much you loved them and what you prayed for them. This is not really a journal for you to express all your thoughts. The frustration or negative feelings we feel that go along with parenting can be expressed in your personal journal or by talking with a friend, spouse, or counselor and in prayer with God. This journal is for you to give as a gift to your child when he or she is grown.

These quiet times with you and your child will cement the bonding process and bring the two of you great peace. Anyone who cares for a child can use this journal- dads, moms, babysitters, foster parents, anyone. And you don't have to be a poet or a writer to use this journal. Any thought, prayer, song, or expression that you have can be jotted down.

Now it's time to begin. Be blessed (empowered to prosper) in this creative work and in this once in a lifetime opportunity to spend time with this child who will be one year old before you know it. What an awesome opportunity to capture memories that you and your child can enjoy for always.

I dedicate this journal to Chandra and Seth, awesome creations from God.

Habakkuk 2:2-3

"Then the Lord answered me and said: Write the vision and make it plain on tablets, that he may run who reads it. For the vision is yet for an appointed time; but at the end it will speak, and it will not lie. Though it tarries, wait for it: because it will surely come, it will not tarry."

This journal is presented to:

_____

At last through my pain,
this human being,
this individual,
bursts forth into my world.
Oh my God!
I am astounded to see the person
who has been so close to me these past months.
So calm and peaceful
and I am so ecstatic.

Luke 2:7 "And she brought forth her firstborn Son, and wrapped Him in swaddling cloths, and laid Him in a manger, because there was no room for them in the inn."

Thought for the day & date:
_____
_____
_____
_____

Pray this for your child: Thank you God for this miracle. Give me wisdom right now and the ability to love this child with Your love.

Small wonder from love's cup of gold, Oh, how I love thee.
The miracle of those tiny hands;
the wonder of the mouth searching for the breast;
the feeling of divine exaltation at child and mother coming together.
My child snuggles as if still in the womb. My senses reel with wonder, love ...like a bird soaring to the inner reaches of ecstasy.
Never have I felt such completeness, such purpose to my existence.

Isaiah 9:6 "For unto us a Child is born, Unto us a Son is given; And the government will be upon His shoulder. And His name will be called Wonderful, Counselor, Mighty God, Everlasting Father, Prince of Peace."

Thought for the day & date:
_____
_____
_____
_____

<u>Pray this for your child</u>: Thank you God for Your perfect work. Bless this child with love and security all the days of her life.

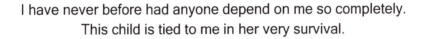

I have never before had anyone depend on me so completely.
This child is tied to me in her very survival.

ME...............

Who am I to think I am able to do this?
How in the world am I ever going to be able to care for this human person in miniature?
Maybe I can't, but God can.
If there ever was a time to pray!

Philippians 4:13 "I can do all things through Christ who strengthens me."

Thought for the day & date:

_____
_____
_____
_____

Pray this for your child: Thank you God that when I am weak, You are strong. You have not given me a spirit of fear. Bless my child with faith and courage to trust You with her life completely.

All I have to give my child is love;
A very pure love and maybe some wisdom
when she is older.
I cannot fill all her needs,
for most times I don't even know
what they are.
All I can be is here, close,
loving, trying and struggling
to understand this little life.

I John 4:18-19 "There is no fear in love; but perfect love casts out fear, because fear has torment. And he who fears has not been made perfect in love. We love Him because He first loved us."

Thought for the day & date:
_____
_____
_____
_____

Pray this for your child: Thank you God that I don't need to have all the answers. Give me wisdom to raise this child the way You would have me do and help me teach this child how to look to You for all her needs.

What an excitement,
as people come to see my baby.

You'd think I made her myself,
from a kit I ordered by mail.

Matthew 2:1-2 "Now after Jesus was born in Bethlehem of Judea in the days of Herod the king, behold, wise men from the East came to Jerusalem, saying, ' Where is He who has been born King of the Jews? For we have seen His star in the East and have come to worship Him.'"

Thought for the day & date:

_____
_____
_____
_____

<u>Pray this for your child</u>: God, my baby is truly a miracle. As she grows help her to know how miraculous birth is and how You see to every detail of life.

In the gray blackness before morning,
I lay here and feel an aching loss through my body.
My stomach feels empty.
That lump that hampered sleep on my stomach for so long, is now gone,
or is it?

As I begin to reach consciousness, for a fleeting moment,
my child is still within and I feel at peace. But no, there is nothing
but sagging emptiness.
As the quiet moments pass, life becomes a half-time pictorial of memories. I grieve for
a while at the loss of this child from my belly.
It becomes starkly apparent how much a part of my life this child really was; or I a
part of hers.
As the child in the crib begins to whimper with awakening, I realize the different reality
of having her here,
and long for the reality of my pregnancy.
The sense of loss will pass as I become accustomed to this new reality.

John 20:11-14 "But Mary stood outside by the tomb weeping, and as she wept she stooped down and looked into the tomb. And she saw two angels in white sitting, one at the head and the other at the feet, where the body of Jesus had lain. Then they said to her, 'Woman, why are you weeping?' She said to them, 'Because they have taken away my Lord, and I do not know where they have laid Him.' Now when she had said this, she turned around and saw Jesus standing there, and did not know that it was Jesus."

Thought for the day & date:

_____
_____
_____
_____

<u>Pray this for your child</u>: God, I know this is just one of the many transitions I and my child will go through. Give us both strength and ability to grow and change.

Sit and look at the wonder of life.

As the days pass,
I find it harder and harder to keep the connection between this child and my pregnancy.
Her reality as an individual is becoming more and more concrete. I also find it hard
to believe
that I could have been allowed to carry anything so beautiful.
Those tiny hands and feet; perfect miniatures of life as I know it
in the adult world.
I feel I've never really noticed a child before. I look and look.
I want to keep every detail of her, at this moment,
etched in my memory forever.
For a moment, I never want her to get older. Could I ever have been so small?
I wonder if my mother studied me, and all my parts,
with the same loving intensity.
I watch the eyes, in that kind of blank stare, before vision becomes clearer, moving,
searching for sight more accurate.
The body; the tiny muscles beneath the skin; the skin so soft; the random movements
that will someday make sense. As my child lives another day,
I am satisfied that I have shared in her wondrous creation completely.

Genesis 1:31 "Then God saw everything that He had made, and indeed it was very good...."

Thought for the day & date:

_____
_____
_____
_____

<u>Pray this for your child</u>: Father, my child is perfectly designed by You.
Thank you

My friends:

"Why she's so small! My baby weighed a lot more." "You're breastfeeding? Are you sure she's getting enough to eat?" "Maybe she cries at night because she's hungry." "I think she cries because she's spoiled!" "You spend too much time with her."

"She's so small!" "She's the smallest baby I've ever seen." "You should leave her alone more……you're spoiling her!" "You mean you put her in bed with you!"

"Don't wash her clothes in that detergent; it's too harsh…..no wonder she has a rash." "What a beautiful baby, so petite; she's all girl!"

My friends?

John 13:34 "A new commandment I give to you, that you love one another; as I have loved you, that you also love one another."

Thought for the day & date:

_____
_____
_____
_____

<u>Pray this for your child</u>: Father God, help me to teach this child how to love You with all of her heart and to love others.

The hubbub is over. The excitement is gone.
All the visitors have left.

Now, I settle down to everyday life.
But life is so different with a child.
The day seems to pass and maybe I've made the bed.
How can I keep the house up, cook meals, have time to myself
and care for this child?

I can't.

I can't do all these things. I find it hard giving up
my homemaker image, but it is so worth it.
She is much more important than that.

I John 2:27 "But the anointing which you have received from Him abides in you, and you do not need that anyone teach you; but as the same anointing teaches you concerning all things, and is true, and is not a lie, and just as it has taught you, you will abide in Him."

Thought for the day & date:
_____
_____
_____
_____

Pray this for your child: As my child grows, dear Father, teach her to rely on You for everything. Thank You.

She really tries to tell me her needs. I know she does.
She has just as much trouble getting herself across to me, in a way I can understand,
as I have, trying to figure out
what it is she is trying to tell me.

We most definitely have a communication problem.

I have no idea how to bridge it.
I can only be here, try to be patient and do what I sense she needs.

Ephesians 6:4 "And you, fathers, do not provoke your children to wrath,
but bring them up in the training and admonition of the Lord."

Thought for the day & date:

_____
_____
_____
_____

<u>Pray this for your child</u>: Father, this child is perfect and I pray that as she grows she develops great wisdom in how to communicate clearly and in how to live each day, depending on You.

So much gratitude over my life permanently changed.
So many thankful moments,
over time not selfishly spent.
So many happy hours,
caring for and loving this child.

So much exhaustion.
So much tiredness.
When will this life settle in?
When will I be content,
juggling so much,
And resting so little?

Galatians 6:7-9 "Do not be deceived, God is not mocked; for whatever a man sows, that will he also reap. For he who sows to his flesh will of the flesh reap corruption, but he who sows to the Spirit will of the Spirit reap everlasting life. And let us not grow weary while doing good, for in due season we shall reap if we do not lose heart."

Thought for the day & date:

_____
_____
_____
_____

<u>Pray this for your child:</u> Father help my child to know at a young age that she can do things in Your strength, not her own. Teach her to see that she can always be refreshed in Your presence.

Laying in my arms....
her eyes finally focusing enough that I am sure she can see me.
I look down occasionally
at that staring face.
What was that!
Wait a minute.....
My mind reels in shock. My life stops.
I stare at her with my smiling face.
Her lips part.....
and she smiles at me!
My God!
My child has smiled at me!
She not only has acknowledged my presence,
but she has connected with me in such a neat way.
My mind and soul take a photo
of this moment
to cherish forever.

This is the fulfillment of the previous verses, Galatians 6:7-9, the reaping!

Thought for the day & date:
_____
_____
_____
_____

<u>Pray this for your child</u>: Father God, teach my child to rejoice in You always.

Several months have passed. When
was the last time my husband and I
were alone?

I can't remember....

I mean really alone, just us.
Alone somewhere,
sharing in each other and
revitalizing our relationship?

Although we have made a place for our child
in our home, in our lives,
we have to be alone occasionally.
I don't want to lose what we have
built up together as just two.
We'll lose a very important part of us.
I feel very anxious about this because
I don't see us getting this time in the near future.

Genesis 2:24 "Therefore a man shall leave his father and mother and be joined to his wife, and they shall become one flesh."

Thought for the day & date:

_____
_____
_____
_____

Pray this: God of heaven who created the union of man and woman, help us to balance our relationship with our family. Give us creative ideas about how to spend time with each other and keep our relationship strong. Let us model a solid husband and wife team to our children. We keep You in the center of our lives.

Boy, it's hard to be on a budget
when you have a new baby.

I go into the store and it seems as though
every toy in the place cries out,
"Take me. Take me. She'd love to have me."

Those moments can always seem comical later,
but at the time, they are far from funny.
At the time, they are painful.

John 14:27 "Peace I leave with you, My peace I give to you; not as the world gives do I give to you. Let not your heart be troubled, neither let it be afraid."

Thought for the day & date:

_____
_____
_____
_____

<u>Pray this for your child</u>: Lord God, help my child to have peace, Your peace, in every situation; teach her to get her peace from You.

My senses fill
with dirty diapers

And a crying child
who can't seem to get settled today.

If I don't get some time alone,
from meals and dirty dishes
and the endless boredom of house cleaning

I'll....
I'll....
I'll.....

Just lie down and cry.

I John 5:14-15 "Now this is the confidence that we have in Him, that if we ask anything according to His will, He hears us. And if we know that He hears us, whatever we ask, we know that we have the petitions that we have asked of Him."

Thought for the day & date:

_____
_____
_____
_____

Pray this for your child: As I need to petition You, Father God, for every need, teach my child to petition You before things get out of hand. Help me model this to my child daily. I thank You for being an ever present help in time of trouble.

My child looks to me with such trusting eyes.....

I could never bring myself to purposely hurt, to displace,
to crush,

That innocent,
Pure,
Simple
Trust.

Proverbs 3:5-6 "Trust in the Lord with all your heart, and lean not on your own understanding; in all your ways acknowledge Him, and He shall direct your paths."

Thought for the day & date:
_____
_____
_____
_____

<u>Pray this for your child:</u> Thank you God that you are totally trustworthy. Help my child to learn this at a very young age and to always trust Your work in her life.

She's growing up……..
The silhouette of her face as she sits on my lap,
is changing,
is maturing.

Her eyes,
as they pierce into mine,
there is thought behind them;
Of what kind I know not.

She's changing before me
in ways I can't keep up with;

But then, aren't mom's at least two steps behind?

Ephesians 4:15 "But, speaking the truth in love, may grow up in all things into Him who is the head-Christ-."

Thought for the day & date:
_____
_____
_____
_____

Pray this for your child: Father God, as she grows, may my child grow in You in every way. Thank you.

Crunch, munch,
Tap, rap,
Flip, flop
Screech, reach,
Grab, stab,
Poke, jab,
Swizzle, kick,
Pound, pick,
What a riot!

Watching my child try to crawl and play.

Galatians 5:22 "But the fruit of the Spirit is love, joy,...."

Thought for the day & date:

_____
_____
_____
_____

<u>Pray this for your child</u>: Let my child, O Lord, display the fruit of joy all the days of her life.

My father once told me,
"People seem to forget that when they have a child
their life changes. They think they can have children
and fit the child into their life.
It doesn't work that way if you are not going
to neglect the child.
Children are individuals and they
may not do things that fit in with your schedule."

I really need to hear those words
because I keep trying to do the reverse.

Philippians 2:4 "Let each of you look out not only for his own interests, but also for the interests of others."

Thought for the day & date:

_____
_____
_____
_____

<u>Pray this for your child</u>: Teach my child, O Lord, to be selfless as she deepens her relationship with You.

Boy, my baby's neat!
How she laughs and tries to imitate
the faces I make at her.

What a little doll face of curiosity,
Love,
Need,
Activity and
Thought.

The miracle of her life still awes me.
I shall never know, although I often guess, what's
happening behind those eyes, wide-eyed and
open to the world.

Isaiah 44:2a "Thus says the Lord who made you, And formed you from the womb, who will help you:…"

Thought for the day & date:
_____
_____
_____
_____

Pray this for your child: Father I pray that my child will worship You and look at Your awesome works with wonder and gratitude.

At nine months, my child is a whirl of life.
Reaching out;
Seeking new and different relationships
with the inanimate
and the human alike.

I feel a pain of losing her;
of longing for a tiny helpless baby again.

Maybe this is the point when mothers
begin to contemplate having
another baby.

I have begun to think in this direction.

Psalm 127:2-5 "Behold, children are a heritage from the Lord. The fruit of the womb is a reward. Like arrows in the hand of a warrior, so are the children of one's youth. Happy is the man who has his quiver full of them."

Thought for the day & date:
_____
_____
_____
_____

Pray this for your child: Father God, I pray that this child and any more children that are coming will know You love them completely and that I love them all very much.

In watching my child play,
I see her doing and acting
in ways I have been with her.

And when I see her...
Yelling and screaming.....

I see me.

Romans 12:2 "And do not be conformed to this world, but be transformed by the renewing of your mind that you may prove what is that good and acceptable and perfect will of God."

Thought for the day & date:

_____
_____
_____
_____

<u>Pray this for your child and yourself</u>: Please help me Lord to stay close to you and to make time for You and for Your Word so that I might be transformed. Protect my child from the parts of me that are not yet renewed. I know You will and I know my child will have every opportunity to be an even better person than I am because of Your boundless love for her.

I would like to write a tribute
to babies everywhere.

They are so neat!

They start out helpless and
little by little they grow
and become more and more independent.

At eleven months
I am truly amazed and awed.
How and where did she learn to do all the
climbing and reaching that she does?

Each movement of leg and arm;
The coordination in her fingers;

The temper!

She carries on a conversation with me.
She has a memory.

So many, many skills and essences of personhood.

I realize again the magnificent creations we all are.

Genesis 1:27 "So God created man in His own image; in the image of God He created him: male and female He created them."

Thought for the day & date:

_____
_____
_____
_____

<u>Pray this for your child</u>: Father God, I pray my child will see You in everything created.

One year old…..

She seems to have changed overnight.
A little girl, no longer a baby
but still very needy of support,
love and encouragement
As she forges into the world

Upright.

Walking seems to change everything.

She can now do what she has watched others do for a year.
Such pride in the expression as she wobbles around the house,
like someone just waking up from a deep sleep.
Such joy and pride with herself at her achievement.
She seems to feel greater insecurity as well.

Her perspective of her world has changed since she is now upright.
Things long familiar from the prone perspective must look very new.

Luke 2:40 "And the Child grew and became strong in spirit, filled with wisdom; and the grace of God was upon Him."

Thought for the day & date:

_____
_____
_____
_____

<u>Pray this for your child</u>: Lord, cause my child to grow and become strong in spirit, and be filled with wisdom and let Your grace be upon my child. Thank you.

Her social attitude has greatly changed.
Such reaching out for people, all people,
any people,
big and small,
male and female.

There is definite lack of awareness
of what to do with these humans
once their attention has been attracted,
but the beginnings to "relating" are there.

Her physical self has changed. She has lost a lot
of "baby fat"; she is longer and leaner.
All the things she attempts to accomplish,
all the complex behaviors like
carrying big objects, unscrewing lids, "loving" her dolls;
it's like suddenly she feels that she is somebody.

I watch me in all this. I struggle to relate to her changes.
I don't want to miss anything. As she changes the way she relates,
I have to learn anew what she is trying to tell me.

I Cor 12:12 "For as the body is one and has many members, but all the members of that one body, being many, are one body, so also is Christ."

Thought for the day & date:

_____
_____
_____
_____

<u>Pray this for your child</u>: Father God, thank You for what You tell us about unity and about diversity. I pray my child will always honor life and difference since we are all one in the body of Christ.

I want to understand.
I want to honor the new found importance she has of herself.
My love is different now. I look back at the
achievement and fear I felt at the little,
helpless person she began.
My love was so tightly wrapped up
in the miracle of new life.

My love and feelings for her now reach
to my depths and have no dimension.
I am awed at her life.
I respect her feelings and right to be.
I feel very separate from her and good about it.
I feel protective.
I feel the beginnings of wanting to share my knowledge.
I seem to want to get further
into this "family" desire of mine,
or rather this choice I have made by which I want to live.

I want a family.

Ephesians 3:14,15a "For this reason I bow my knees to the Father of our Lord Jesus Christ, from whom the whole family in heaven and earth is named,......"

Thought for the day & date:

_____
_____
_____
_____

<u>Pray this for your child</u>: God in heaven, help my child to know that she is part of a large family, the family of God, and that she belongs and is accepted completely.

I feel a deep love that I want to give.
That love is just there, tender and sure.

More than that, what has been growing,
for months now, is a profound awe and respect
that soars beyond the boundaries
of my comprehension - - -

Of the miracle and the brilliance
of every human being,
Who start out in life so dependent,
but who demand the right to be.

Let us protect this right
of creation.
Let us not
make skyscrapers out of
morning glories.

I John 4:10,11 "In this is love, not that we loved God, but that He loved us and sent His Son to be the propitiation for our sins. Beloved, if God so loved us, we also ought to love one another."

Thought for the day & date:
_____
_____
_____
_____

<u>Pray this for your child</u>: Help my child, dear Lord, to understand Your great love for her and mankind. Plant within her Your love for others.

Additional Thoughts/Prayers/Mementos for my child:
Date:
Time:
Thought/Prayer/Memento:

Additional Thoughts/Prayers/Mementos for my child:
Date:
Time:
Thought/Prayer/Memento:

Additional Thoughts/Prayers/Mementos for my child:
Date:
Time:
Thought/Prayer/Memento:

Psalm 139:13-16

"You made all the delicate, inner parts of my body and knit me together in my mother's womb. Thank you for making me so wonderfully complex! Your workmanship is marvelous— how well I know it. You watched me as I was being formed in utter seclusion, as I was woven together in the dark of the womb. You saw me before I was born.

Every day of my life was recorded in your book.

Every moment was laid out before a single day had passed."

Printed in the USA
CPSIA information can be obtained
at www.ICGtesting.com
LVHW060931081224
798622LV00015B/1029